FIRST, A WORD FROM THE AUTHOR...

Thanks for picking up the book, I hope it turns out to be everything you want it to be. Green snakes are fascinating creatures. Your average herpetologist or herpetoculturist will think all snakes are, of course, but since there are so

Green snakes don't really fall into the "overlooked" category, at least not in the commercial sense. They do appear in pet stores on a fairly regular basis (if they didn't, I don't think this book would exist), but they are routinely dismissed by most herpers as

PHOTO OF THE SMOOTH GREEN SNAKE, *OPHEODRYS VERNALIS*, BY JOHN DOMMERS

Green snakes, while rarely captive-bred, have always been a pet-shop staple. Most specimens will take live crickets without fuss, making them easy, enjoyable captives.

many species, most tend to somehow get "lost in the mix."

Think about it this way—there are well over 2500 snake species, yet only about 100 of them, at the *most*, are ever seen in the pet trade. That's less than *three percent*. Think of how many intriguing creatures there must be in that remaining 97%. It's mind-boggling, isn't it?

"kids' snakes" or "beginners' snakes." This is unfair. Admittedly, green snakes are low-priced, easy to house and feed, simple-colored, and very benevolent. Perfect for the budding hobbyist, but too easy for the pros, right?

Perhaps, but, as the saying goes, beauty is in the eye of beholder. I received a phone call

PHOTO BY W. P. MARA

There are two species of North American green snake—the Smooth Green, *Opheodrys vernalis*, and the Rough Green, *Opheodrys aestivus*, which is shown here. *Aestivus* is the more common of the two as far as commercial availability is concerned.

not more than a month ago from a nice fellow who sounded like he was in his mid-thirties. He professed a deep love for green snakes and said he'd been keeping and breeding them for ages. In my opinion, this guy really knows what it's all about. He doesn't care what everyone else thinks. He likes them and that's all that matters.

And that's all that should matter to you. If you've suddenly found yourself attracted to these wonderful animals, you should follow that infatuation to its logical conclusion—set up a tank and keep a few. A book on the subject will help you with your endeavors, and that's why this one was written. I've tried to include a little bit of everything—

feeding, breeding, housing, natural history, etc. It's more of a keeper's guide than anything else, but there are sections on behavior in the wild, identification characteristics, the complexities of green snake taxonomy, and so on. 'Look no further,' I want this book to say, 'for all your answers will be found within.' It is that sense of "completeness" that gives a reader his or her greatest sense of security.

Once again, I sincerely hope it lives up to your expectations. (Oh, and if you're trying to read it in the store so you don't have to pay for it, I hope the store manger catches you and throws you out.)

Good luck.

W. P. Mara

ACKNOWLEDGMENTS

I'd like to give thanks to Jerry G. Walls for sharing his wealth of *Opheodrys* literature with me. His thoughtfulness and consideration (not to mention the physical effort required to dig through his vast personal library) really made a difference in the overall manuscript. Gratitude in this case should be as much the reader's as it is mine.

DEDICATION

And this one I dedicate to Dr. Hobart M. Smith, my friend, for "paving many roads and lighting many torches."

The snakes of the genus *Opheodrys* are strictly North American. They occur mainly in the United States, but there also are populations in northern Mexico (to Tampico and Coahuila) and southern Canada. Shown is the Smooth Green Snake, *Opheodrys vernalis*.

PHOTO BY WILLIAM B. ALLEN, JR.

PHOTO OF A ROUGH GREEN SNAKE, *OPHEODRYS AESTIVUS*, BY W. P. MARA

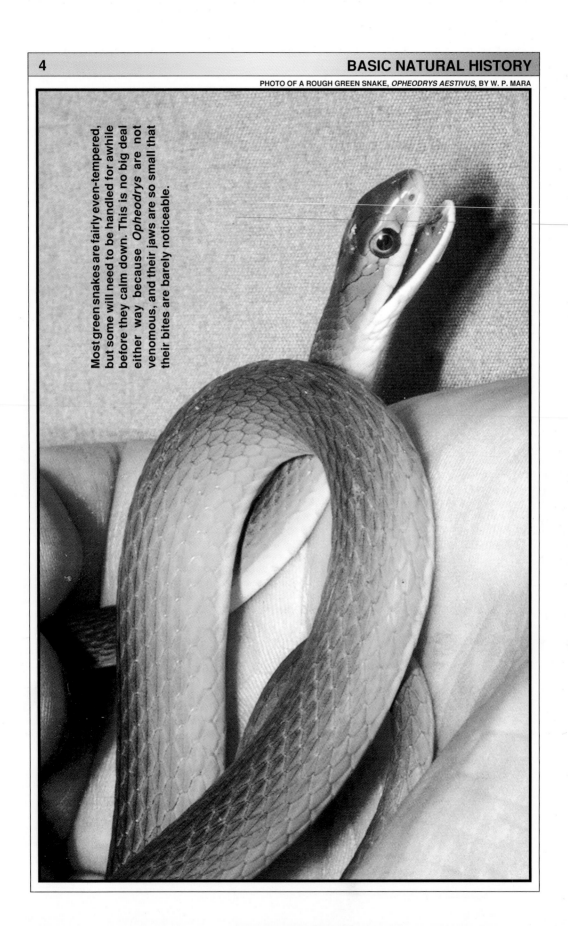

Most green snakes are fairly even-tempered, but some will need to be handled for awhile before they calm down. This is no big deal either way because *Opheodrys* are not venomous, and their jaws are so small that their bites are barely noticeable.

BASIC NATURAL HISTORY OF THE GENUS *OPHEODRYS*

TAXONOMY

The taxonomy of the green snakes is somewhat strange and a bit messy (is taxonomy ever anything else?). Not only are taxonomists incapable of reaching an agreement on how many subspecies there are, they can't even decide how many *species* there are. In fact, it is believed by some that the *Opheodrys* occurring in the United States really constitute more than one *genus*. Whew!

Serpentes (snakes and lizards), the suborder Squamata (snakes), and the family Colubridae (typical snakes). The genus *Opheodrys* often is thought of as encompassing the two green snakes species in the United States. The "first" species, *aestivus*, known in English as the Rough Green Snake, was first described by Linnaeus in 1766. The second, *vernalis*, known as the Smooth Green Snake, was described by Harlan in 1827.

PHOTO BY W. P. MARA

The scales of the Rough Green Snake, *Opheodrys aestivus*. Notice the conspicuous keeling, which is not present in the Smooth Green Snake, *O. vernalis*. This characteristic is one easy way to tell the two species apart.

Okay, let's start with the basics. The green snakes discussed in this book (two species only) belong in the phylum Chordata (backboned animals), the class Reptilia (reptiles), the order

Some taxonomists believe *Opheodrys* is not strictly a North American genus, but rather that more species occur in Asia. I'm not going to get into the subtleties of how and why this conclusion exists, but suffice it to say the *Opheodrys* types in Asia are similar enough in morphology to arouse suspicion.

Nevertheless, other taxonomists are hard-pressed to believe two groups of snakes so far apart can be of the same genus, and I tend to agree. Perhaps at one time they *were* of the same group, but that was quite a long time ago, and taxonomy, in all its man-made superficiality, needs to keep pace with evolution. Thus, the Asian species that once were thought to be *Opheodrys* now belong in a handful of "new" genera.

The other problem lies in the subject of subspecies. One view is that both *aestivus* and *vernalis* are monotypic, meaning they have no subspecies, but the other view (which seems slightly more popular) is that *vernalis* has two—*O. v. vernalis* (Eastern Smooth Green Snake) and *O. v. blanchardi* (Western Smooth Green Snake). There even is a paper by Arnold B. Grobman (Bull. Fla. St. Mus.; Vol. 29, No.

The belly of the Rough Green Snake, *Opheodrys aestivus*. The belly color of both green snakes is more or less uniform. In most cases, it is white to pale yellow, but on some Rough Green specimens it may be a very pale green.

PHOTO BY W. P. MARA

PHOTO OF A SMOOTH GREEN SNAKE, *O. VERNALIS*, BY R. T. ZAPPALORTI

Depending on which taxonomist you talk to, you may find there either are quite a number of green snake subspecies or none at all. Taxonomy and systematics are tricky and sometimes highly subjective scientific disciplines that easily could take up an entire book of their own.

3; "Scutellation Variation in *Opheodrys aestivus*") in which even *aestivus* has four. Jeez! Where does it end?!

How about this—since the main focus of this book is on husbandry rather than taxonomy (and since I'm not a taxonomist and therefore not trying to present an opinion), I'm not going to get into which views I believe are correct. In the case of *vernalis*, both "forms," shall we say, have virtually identical husbandry, and the same goes for all four "forms" of *aestivus*, and that's good enough for me. For the remainder of this book I'm going to treat green snakes on the species level and no deeper. If you really want to delve further into the issue, get your hands on a good field guide and contact some professional herpetologists who deal with such things. By gathering as much data as possible, you will grant yourself a clear overview of the whole problem and in turn be able to form an opinion of your own.

IDENTIFICATION

Superficially, both the Rough and the Smooth Green Snake look exactly as their genus's common name implies—green, nothing more and nothing less. The shade is a fairly bright one, like that of a healthy lawn. Of course, there is more to properly identifying a snake than knowing its dorsal color.

The belly, for example, is, on both species, a different color than the dorsum. On the Rough Green Snake it is white, yellow, or a very pale, very diluted green, whereas on the Smooth Green Snake the belly is a white or a very washed-out yellow. Hints of the belly color can be seen on the lowest lateral scales when the

A beautiful specimen of the Smooth Green Snake, *Opheodrys vernalis*, from Sussex County, New Jersey. New Jersey is one of the few states that harbors both *Opheodrys* species. Photo by R. T. Zappalorti.

snake is situated normally.

Interestingly, both green snakes will turn a very pretty bluish color immediately after death; a fact that somehow manages to be fascinating in spite of its morbidty. I cannot fully explain this phenomenon, but it truly is a sight to behold (although I don't advise the premeditated murder of one's snakes just to experience it). Similarly, any damaged areas of skin also turn blue for a short time.

Neonates also are mono-colored on both dorsum and ventrum, but neither's appearance is indicative of their respective parents. Newborns of the Rough Green Snake are grayish green, and those of the Smooth Green are olive-green or gray with a suggestion of dark blue. This makes both neonates a little duller than their parents, which is interesting when you note that the neonates of almost every other snake species in the world are considerably brighter in color than their parents. It sort of is the "rule" with snakes. Also, neonatal green snakes have relatively larger eyes, longer heads, and smaller tails than adults.

To say the green snakes are slender-bodied would be an understatement. Even the largest (fattest?) specimens aren't much thicker than an ordinary pencil. They are, however, fairly long for such thin snakes. Average length for the Rough Green is about 22 to 32 in/56 to 81 in. The record, according to Conant and Collins's *A Field Guide to Reptiles and Amphibians, Eastern and Central*

North America, is 45.6 in/115.9 cm. The Smooth Green is a little shorter, reaching an average adult length of around 12 to 20 in/30 to 51 cm, and the record there is 26

One physical characteristic the green snakes are known for is a slender body. It helps them glide through busy networks of leaves and branches and also aids them in their camouflage efforts. Photo by B. Kahl.

in/66 cm. Notably, both green snakes have tails that constitute almost half their total length. The head of the Rough Green is fairly elongated, offset, and possessing a prominent snout, whereas that of the Smooth Green is comparatively shorter, stouter, and rounded at the nose. Coloration of the chin and lower labials often is lighter than that of the belly.

In order to really get down to the finer points of external identification, you have to involve yourself with scalation. This can be a tedious and frustrating task since most snakes generally don't care to sit still while their bodies are being scrutinized. Nevertheless, the information can be useful.

Green snakes have divided anal plates (the anal plate is located on the posterior portion of the belly; it covers the cloacal vent and separates the "main" portion of a snake's body from the tail). The dorsal scales are either keeled (Rough Green, hence its common name) or smooth (Smooth Green, same deal). Number of scale rows should be either 15 (Rough Green) or 17 (Smooth Green), with a ventral scale count of 148 to 166 for the Rough and 116 to 154 for the Smooth, and a caudal (tail) scale count of 110 to 148 for the Rough and 116 to 154 for the smooth.

GEOGRAPHY

The green snakes are fairly widespread over the eastern half of the United States. They also occur in Canada and Mexico, but the aforementioned eastern U. S. makes up the bulk of their range.

To really get down to the finer points of green snake identification, you need to do scale counts. The problem is most live snakes usually won't sit still long enough for you to do this! Shown is a Smooth Green Snake, *Opheodrys vernalis*.

PHOTO BY R. T. ZAPPALORTI

They occur as far north as the Maritime Provinces of Canada and southeastern Saskatchewan (Smooth Green); as far west as central Utah (Smooth Green); south to Tampico, Mexico, with an isolated population in Coahuila (Rough Green); and east along the Coastal Plains/eastern shores from Florida right up into Maine and beyond (Rough in the southern areas, Smooth in the north).

HABITAT

According to virtually all written accounts, green snakes occur in a vast variety of habitats. Those listed include flatwoods, wooded rocky hillsides, forest glades, tree savannah, prairielands, palmetto ridges, wooded canyons, sphagnum bogs, vine tangles, hedgerows, marshes, quiet ponds, and uncultivated fields, just to name a few. The list could of course go on, but the point already has been established. The one constant seems to be a reasonable proximity to water. Green snakes have been referred to on more than one occassion as "edge" snakes, meaning they often are found along the edge of watercourses. One author even went so far as to suggest they seem semi-aquatic at certain times, further noting that green snakes are excellent swimmers and may voluntarily enter the water at any time.

HABITS

Anyone who has firsthand experience with both green snake species probably has noticed one distinct difference between them—the Rough Green is devotedly arboreal while the Smooth Green almost never leaves the ground (although, interestingly, even the Rough Green becomes more terrestrial during the spring and fall). In nature, unsurprisingly, the situation is much the same. Rough Greens routinely are seen gliding through shrubs, dense shoreline vegetation, vine tangles, and so on, and in cases where they haunt flora with much green coloring, they become nearly invisible. (On a fascinating side note, when a Rough Green is camouflaged in this way and a strong wind comes along and causes the foliage of waver, the snake also will waver to maintain the illusion.) Smooth Greens, on the other hand, have almost always been found on the ground, usually under leaf litter, stones, boards, and so on (although there are exceptional reports of Smooth Greens taking to small trees or bushes).

Green snakes are diurnal, often foraging on even the warmest days. They are remarkably mild-tempered, even when first grasped in the wild, but still may be a little squirmy. They are alert and intelligent, hunting in shrubs or tall grasses with their heads raised to gain a better survey of their immediate area. They do not constrict their food, but rather grasp it in their jaws and gulp it down or crush it first and then gulp it down.

REPRODUCTION

Green snakes are oviparous, meaning they lay eggs rather than give birth to live young (snakes of the latter variety are termed *viviparous*). They mate in both spring and fall, but egglaying occurs almost always in summer, after the spring breedings (obviously, since a green snake that has mated in the fall is not going to lay eggs in the winter). Normal egg clutch size is between three and 12, the average being around five or six. The eggs are capsule-shaped and measure about 1.5 in/2.8 cm in length. Those of the Rough Green are rather tough whereas those of the Smooth Green are somewhat softer. Both Rough and Smooth Greens are known to lay their eggs in communal nests. Reported egglaying sites include inside moist moss beds, under or in rotting logs, inside rotting railroad ties, under pieces of wet cardboard, inside piles of decaying leaves, under large flat rocks, and one worker even found a group clutch inside the walls of an old refrigerator.

One major difference between *aestivus* and *vernalis* lies in the duration of egg incubation. Eggs of the Rough Green normally take anywhere from five to 12 weeks to hatch, whereas those of the Smooth Green can hatch in as little as four *days* (normal maximum only *23* days). This is one of the shortest egg-incubation periods of any snake in the world.

Newborns are frightfully small, usually measuring no more than 8 in/20.3 cm for the Rough Green and 6.5 in/16.5 for the Smooth. They look like blades of dark grass (albeit fat, cylindrical, and squirmy blades of grass with flicking forked tongues and a pair of tiny eyes. Okay, so maybe it wasn't such a good analogy after all). The young grow fairly quickly, reaching sexual maturity in 24 months or less.

Green snakes have very small egg clutches—more than eight eggs in one clutch is quite unusual. The norm is somewhere around five or six.

PHOTO BY ISABELLE FRANCAIS

HOUSING

Setting up a home for a green snake is a piece of cake. These animals live in so many different environments and are so adaptable to varying climates that there's very little a keeper really has to worry about. Some snakes have very specific requirements, like precise temperatures and humidity levels, but not the green snakes. There are, of course, certain general standards that must be observed, but that applies to the keeping of any living thing (including yourself).

CORRECT SIZE AND SHAPE OF THE ENCLOSURE

Green snakes are, as you already know if you read the natural history section, relatively small. I always like to think of relative snake-sizes in these terms—snakes that grow up to six or seven feet are small, those from around seven feet to around ten are moderate, and those over ten are large. Something like the Reticulated Python, *Python reticulatus*, which grows up to 25 feet on a regular basis, should be considered more of a monster than a pet. An animal like that could have two zip codes!

But as I said, green snakes are small so they're not going to need a huge enclosure. Once again, this is to the keeper's advantage since large enclosures are alarmingly *expensive*. In my opinion, a pair of adult green

Single adult green snake specimens can be kept in a 10-gallon enclosure. Adult pairs, however, particularly those you plan to breed, should be kept in a '20.' Notice the components of this simple setup—a rock, a hidebox, a waterbowl, and a paper-towel substrate. The Rough Green Snake inside has everything it needs.

snakes can be housed comfortably in a 20-gallon glass aquarium, which can be purchased at virtually any pet shop. It obviously would be nicer for the snakes if you gave them a larger enclosure, but a "20" is the minimum.

Shape of the tank is important because each of the two green snake species will require something different. The Rough Green, which is primarily arboreal, will need a "high" tank rather than a "long" one, whereas the Smooth Green, being terrestrial, will get more use out of the "long" than the "high." The aforementioned 20-gallon glass tank is offered in

PHOTO BY W. P. MARA

both "high" and "long" models, as are those of other sizes. Of course, if you decide to go nuts and purchase something colossal like a 55-gallon or a 70-gallon tank, then you really don't have to be too concerned with height and length in the first place. (The other advantage to this is that you can keep both species in the same enclosure.)

COMPONENTS AND FURNISHINGS

Substrates

For anyone who doesn't know what the word means in the herpetocultural context, a substrate is a bedding used to cover the floor of an enclosure. The carpeting in your house is a substrate, as is the sand on an ocean floor.

The question becomes, 'Which substrate is the best for green snakes?' Answer—the word "best" will be defined differently by each keeper because each keeper has different needs. Some, for example, love to set up highly detailed naturalistic enclosures whereas others can't be bothered with such complicated undertakings. Of course, the former attitude usually changes to the latter after a keeper has earned his or her the third hernia from lugging around glass aquariums filled with soil and large rocks.

It probably would be best simply to discuss some of the more common substrates and present both positive and negative aspects of each. From there you should be able to

If you have the time, space, patience, and skill, you might consider building an elaborate, full-blown aquaterrarium setup like this one; a colony of green snakes would love it. You could keep other herptiles in it as well (provided, of course, they were socially compatible with the green snakes).

PHOTO BY R. G. SPRACKLAND

figure out which one best suits your needs.

For the keeper who insists on naturalistic setups, and in regards to our friends the green snakes, there are three good substrate choices available.

Potting soil is a logical first choice. Bags of it can be purchased in many places (don't take any from your backyard because you don't know what's crawling around in it). Soil is fairly easy to work with,

Setting up a green snake enclosure requires only a small amount of time and effort. As long as you have the essentials—a substrate, a waterbowl, a rock, a climbing branch, and the proper climate—your snake(s) will do fine.

inexpensive, and allows for the inclusion of live plants. The main problem with potting soil is that it tends to be messy. When I was bothering with naturalistic setups, one of my goals was visual esthetics, i.e., I wanted things to look nice. Well, it didn't take long for me to realize a glass tank full of potting soil and a few snakes soon turned into a glass box with gritty brown smears on every wall and a mud puddle in the waterbowl.

The next option is gravel. It is attractive, can be bought at most pet shops, and is reusable. The downside is the same as with sand—a gravel-filled glass aquarium is alarmingly heavy.

Lastly, bark mulch and bark nuggets are popular beddings. Both have their advantages. They can be bought in bulk, are easy on your back (lightweight), look nice, and green snakes seem to approve of them. A problem, though, is that they lend themselves to the spread of disease organisms. Occasionally a bag turns up that is already infected or infested, and it won't take long for your snakes to become victims.

Regardless of which natural substrate you use, be sure to put in plenty of it because both green snake species like to burrow every now and then. A layer about three inches deep is recommended.

Moving on to the "artificial" stuff, some paper products, like newspapers and paper towels, seem to work well. Newspaper costs nothing (if you hang around recycling bins) and can be thrown out when soiled. The main drawback is the unsightliness (plus the fact that some people think newspaper ink is harmful to snakes, although I've never personally seen any evidence of this). Paper towels, my personal choice, can be bought uncolored (uninked), are very easy to work with, and are quite absorbent. They also are very, *very* safe for your snakes.

The last "artificial" substrate I'll endorse is indoor/outdoor carpeting. Lengths of this can be purchased at many pet shops (in pre-cut sizes to fit most glass aquariums). Advantages include the fact that it is very light, reusable, and actually looks kind of nice. Available colors include earthy brown and green. Both look nice when set under a few rocks, branches, and a potted plant or two.

You will need to use a few rocks to keep indoor/outdoor carpeting in place because your snakes will want to crawl under it. Also keep in mind indoor/outdoor carpeting starts to fall apart after it's been washed about 40 or 50 times, and really strong smells seem to linger forever.

Rocks

There should be a few rocks in just about any snake's enclosure. The essential purpose of a rock is to provide a snake with a rough surface on which to begin a shed. Unshed skin can cause skin infections and possible blindness in the case of adherent eye caps (brilles).

Even if you've chosen to set up a "clinical" enclosure (paper towels, a plastic waterbowl, and hidebox, etc.), you should include at least one rock. In the case of naturalistic setups, a few rocks will add beauty to the overall tableaux.

You can find rocks almost anywhere. Some pet stores carry attractive examples, but if you can't find any in your local shop, check out a landscaper's supply house or a garden center. If that also proves fruitless, explore a tract of undeveloped land.

Waterbowls

All snakes need water, and most will take it right from a bowl. It is important for the bowl to have a wide base so it can't be overturned. If you can't find such a waterbowl, use one that is very heavy, like a ceramic bowl. Green snakes do like to swim occasionally, so make sure the bowl is of fairly good size. Also, for the sake of cleanliness and your snakes' health, change the water every other day (at *least*), washing the bowl out thoroughly before refilling it.

Hideboxes

A snake that is not given a place to hide will become stressed and eventually may die as a result. Like humans, snakes occasionally need to be left alone.

Hide*box* is a misleading word because a snake's hiding area need not strictly be a box. Some people have used plastic food containers with holes cut through the lid, cork logs, and even wadded up newspaper. The key, of course, is to make sure the animal feels secure. Don't let a lot of light get inside, and don't routinely remove the hidebox when the animal's in it. You can make hideboxes from plastic shoe or sweaterboxes, or you can make use of more naturalistic materials like a group of rocks cemented together. Don't fall prey to the "I'll just pile a bunch of rocks on top of each other until I've got a cave" approach or you may end up with dead snakes that were unfortunate enough to be inside the cave when it collapsed.

Plants and Branches

Plants and branches fulfill two purposes. They add a touch of naturalism, and they provide objects for your snakes to climb on. Obviously this latter point will be more appreciated by the arboreal Rough Green Snake rather than the more terrestrial Smooth Green.

If you're aiming for a clinical setup rather than one that is naturalistic, you'll want to put in only one or two branches at the most. If, on the other hand, you're aiming to maintain a cubic parcel of nature in a glass box, then I advise you to go completely overboard! Set up a full-blown terrarium! Horticulture is a fun and fascinating pastime all its own.

Here's a helpful word of warning about branches—you may have trouble getting them

PHOTO BY M. P. AND C. PIEDNOIR

Green snakes, particularly the Rough Green, *Opheodrys aestivus*, need branches to climb on. Without them, most greens will become highly stressed and probably die. The Smooth Green, *O. vernalis*, is slightly more terrestrial, but it still takes to the air on occasion.

completely clean. Even if you can remove dried feces from the surface of the wood, that won't guarantee cleanliness below the surface. Sandpaper may help remove some stuff, but, again, the germs that sink into the wood still won't be eliminated.

CONTROLLING THE CLIMATE

Heat

Green snakes need heat. During the warmer parts of the year you may be able to provide this simply by opening the window in the snake room. In colder months, however, you will have to provide heat by some artificial means. The ideal temperature for a green snake is somewhere around 80°F/26°C.

There are a number of items that provide heat. A particularly efficient one is the undertank heating pad. Many keepers like undertank pads because they warm only a single area, affording the snake or snakes the freedom to move onto or

PHOTO COURTESY OF FOUR PAWS

Your local pet shop will offer a wide range of heat sources for your green snakes. Heated rocks and caves are adequate for the interior of your tank, and undertank heaters will warm the overall habitat.

away from that area at will. Also, undertank heating pads can be used without any dissension to tank security (i.e., you don't have to run an electrical cord under the tank's lid).

I can give you one helpful hint concerning heating pads. There are some that are supposed to stick to the bottom of the tank, but the adherent substance is so incredibly adherent that you'll never be able to get the pad off again. Here's the solution—wrap the pad in tin foil. All you have to do from then on is slip it under the tank when you want to use it and slip it back out when you're done.

A second heating item is a spot lamp, which, when aimed at a particular area, will create a basking spot. Heat lamps are sold at many pet shops. They can be used with many herptiles, not just snakes.

Finally, there's ambient heat, usually provided by a small single-room heater. Ambient heat fulfills the needs of many keepers, particularly those who have many tanks since buying a heating pad or heat lamp for each enclosure will drain your wallet in no time flat. Ceramic heaters are inexpensive both to

PHOTO BY ISABELLE FRANCAIS

A green snake will no doubt enjoy having this much leafy green cover in its enclosure. The keeper, however, may not see the animal very often! Photo by Isabelle Francais.

purchase and to run. Set one up with a thermostat (some have thermostats already built in) and you're ready to roll. The only bad part about providing heat in this fashion is if the surrounding temperature in a snake's enclosure gets too warm, the animal(s) can escape it only by going into its waterbowl.

Lighting (Photoperiod)

"Photoperiod" often is defined as "the amount of daylight an animal is exposed to." Concerning green snakes, the amount of daylight provided should be around 12 hours per day during the active season, then growing shorter as autumn approaches.

An easy way to make sure your snakes get the correct photoperiod is to hook up your lighting apparatus to a timer. This obviously will relieve you of the responsibility of turning the lights on and off yourself. Timers can be purchased at most any department store, hardware store, or home-improvement center. The quality of the light need only be ordinary tungsten. Many people who keep turtles and lizards know what a "full-spectrum" light bulb does—it replicates the quality of light given off by the sun. Its main purpose is to aid a turtle or a lizard in the production of vitamin D_3, which both need in order to survive.

Green snakes, however, don't need full-spectrum light, which is good news for you since full-

Providing your green snake with the correct photoperiod (day/night cycle) is very important. Photoperiod is often a factor in determining a herptile's behaviorisms. Bulbs designed specifically for the keeping of reptiles and amphibians now are available at many pet shops.

PHOTO COURTESY OF ENERGY SAVERS

PHOTO COURTESY OF OCEAN NUTRITION

Keeping an eye on the ambient temperature and humidity of your green snake's enclosure is an important facet of good husbandry. If the animal is allowed to become too warm or too moist (or either of the opposites), it could become ill. Fortunately, thermometers and hygrometers designed specifically for herp-keeping are now available.

spectrum bulbs are expensive. It is worth mentioning, however, that some breeders have claimed that snakes exposed to full-spectrum lighting for about five or six hours per day have better breeding results than snakes kept under ordinary light. The improvement seems to lie in the snakes' willingness to breed, the hardiness of the eggs, and the size of the clutch. In the end, the fact is a little full-spectrum lighting won't really harm your snakes one way or another.

A Note on Moisture and Humidity

In spite of the fact that green snakes rarely stray far from water in the wild, they do need to be kept relatively dry in captivity. In other words, no daily spray-mistings are required here, nor is giving attention to retaining moisture. Green snakes are highly susceptible to skin blisters, so keep their cages fairly dry. The only way they should be able to get wet is by bathing in their waterbowls.

CLEANING THE ENCLOSURE

It is vital that a hobbyist keep his or her green snakes' enclosure clean. A thorough cleaning should be performed *at*

PHOTO BY ISABELLE FRANCAIS

Cleanliness of a green snake's enclosure is perhaps the keeper's greatest responsibility. It is something that must be attended to with discipline and devotion. Green snakes forced to live in filthy enclosures rarely live long.

PHOTO BY ISABELLE FRANCAIS

A cursory cleaning should be performed each time you spot fecal matter, and a more thorough cleaning (a "complete" cleaning) should be performed once every two weeks *at least*. Remember, snakes can't clean their own enclosures; *you have to do it for them*.

least once a week. A filthy enclosure will promote all sorts of nasty little health problems. The keys to avoiding them are 1) making sure your pets are being given a steady and nutritional diet, and 2) making sure their surroundings are *as clean as possible.*

Use this simple, step-by-step method of cleaning a snake's enclosure (in this case a glass tank) and you should have no problems. I've used it for many years, and the results always have been satisfying.

1) Take the occupants out of the enclosure and place them in a secure holding area. Try a deep plastic bucket or garbage can with a tight-fitting lid.

2) Remove all climate-control equipment. This includes heating devices, lights, and so on. Since these items use electricity, they should be kept well away from the tank, which soon will be filled with water.

3) Remove all other components. Disposing of the disposables (wood shavings, paper towels, etc.), and placing the reusables in a bucket.

4) Cleanse the empty tank thoroughly using a mixture of warm water, dish soap, and a splash of household bleach. The bleach takes care of all the really nasty germs, while the soap does more of the superficial cleaning. Use a sponge or an old rag, but not a scrub pad for it will scratch the glass. If you have any stubbornly adherent matter, let it soak in the water/soap/ bleach mixture for a few

minutes. If that doesn't help, carefully chip it off the big pieces a plastic knife, then moisten the remaining filthy spot until it softens.

5) Rinse the tank in cold water, and rinse it well. The last thing a snake needs is bleach residue on its skin. Also be sure the tank is *completely dry.*

6) Now clean the reusable items (except those made of wood) using the same procedure outlined in steps four and five. Wood items can be cleaned by scraping away large pieces of fecal matter and then sanding the remaining spot with a sheet of medium-grade sandpaper.

7) Set up the enclosure again.

8) Now you either can place the snakes back into their enclosure, or you can bathe them and *then* stick them back in their enclosure. Does the idea of bathing a snake sound strange? It shouldn't. Consider the fact that snakes get fecal matter on themselves just as easily as they do on everything else. Also consider that skin infections can develop. Bathing a snake gives its keeper the chance to inspect it, looking for early signs of illness, abrasions, cuts, scars, skinniness, and things like that. I like to think of it as a weekly health inspection.

A sensible bathing procedure doesn't involve any kind of soaps, powders, or perfumes. All you really need to do is fill up a little tub with some warm water, slosh the snakes around in it for a few minutes, then dry them with a soft towel.

PHOTO BY ISABELLE FRANCAIS

When setting up a quarantine or temporary holding enclosure, paper products such as newspaper or paper toweling make good beddings.

PHOTO BY ISABELLE FRANCAIS

A green snake's waterbowl often is the place where pathogens meet to multiply. Thus, it is vital that you give the bowl a thorough cleaning and refill it with fresh water at least every other day.

FEEDING

Perhaps the only problem a keeper of green snakes is ever likely to encounter is a wild-caught adult specimen's refusal to feed. Inappetence is common with *many* wild-caught adult herptiles and probably arises from the fact that they simply cannot adjust to an environment so radically different from the one in which they have spent their entire lives. The only other times a green snake will steadfastly refuse food are when it is sick, in the middle of a shedding cycle, or gravid.

FOOD ITEMS

The diet of the green snakes is both simple and inexpensive, which, again, is of great benefit to the keeper. For the most part, they are insectivorous, meaning they dine almost entirely on insects.

CRICKETS

Crickets probably are the most beloved food of the green snakes. Best of all, they offer complete nutrition. They can be purchased in quantity at your local pet shop or can be ordered in bulk quantities from a few professional cricket breeders. For the casual keeper, the pet store choice is better because you only have to buy what you need at that particular moment. A pet store will gladly sell you ten crickets, but a breeder usually only sells in quantities of 500 or more. That means you will not only have to care for your amphibians, but for their food as well, and sometimes this

Increase the nutritional value of your green snakes' food items by powdering them with a little calcium powder during every third or fourth feeding.

PHOTO COURTESY OF AMERICAN REPTILE

PHOTO BY MARK SMITH

Some wild crickets (like the *Acheta gryllus* shown above) can be collected from the field and fed to your green snakes. However, it ultimately is better to buy domestically cultured crickets (below/*Acheta domestica*) because wild ones may be have been exposed to pesticide treatment.

PHOTO BY ISABELLE FRANCAIS

BOTH PHOTOS BY W. P. MARA

As you no doubt will realize after acquiring your first specimen, most green snakes are efficient and enthusiastic hunters. Unlike many other snakes, they are not constrictors. Instead, they simply grab a food item in their jaws, crush it (when necessary), and swallow it down. This whole procedure rarely takes more than a few seconds.

One problem you'll have to watch out for after your green snake grows accustomed to captive living is obesity. Some green snakes are fussy and stubborn at first, but after they pass this stage they are downright voracious. This specimen, a beautiful example of the Rough Green Snake, *Opheodrys aestivus*, that was kept by the author, still takes over a dozen crickets per feeding! Photo by W. P. Mara.

can be more difficult than caring for the pets themselves!

Crickets are easy to maintain. Keep them in a 10-gallon glass tank with a bedding of potting soil. Make sure the lid is aerated so moisture doesn't build up. The reason for the tall tank (10s aren't particularly tall to the human eye, but they sure are to a cricket's!) is so the crickets can't jump out when you lift the lid. I once loaded a bunch of them into a plastic sweaterbox, and the first time I took the top off about fifty of them leaped out. The reason for the soil bedding is so the females can lay their eggs anywhere they wish (and they will, believe me). Hiding places can be provided via a few cardboard paper-towel tubes (or the smaller toilet-paper tubes) plus some egg-carton sections. Food can be offered in shallow plastic dishes, as can water (a water-soaked sponge resting in a small puddle works very well). Common foods include mashed fruits (apples, oranges, etc.), crush oats or bran (uncooked oatmeal, corn flakes), and a sprinkling of multivitamin powder. The enclosure should be cleaned once every two weeks, and the water and food checked daily. The sponge will dry up rather quickly, so have a plastic bottle filled with water on hand. The food may spoil and become moldy, so keep and eye on that too. Put in a new helping of food every fifth day.

Once a green snake gets going on a routine feeding schedule, you can begin to vary its diet. You might want to give it crickets other than those of the standard domestic form. This one, for example, is the Camel Cricket.

PHOTO BY MARK SMITH

PHOTO BY DAVID J. ZOFFER

Some green snakes will accept mealworms, which can be purchased in quantity at most pet shops.

Before you even get involved in green snake keeping, make sure you are able to continually supply tiny crickets to young specimens. I once ended up with a clutch of eggs from a Rough Green, and when those babies hatched, I went crazy trying to find food for them. I eventually succeeded, and therefore the babies lived, but the stress of trying to locate a supplier on a moment's notice was so stressful it almost killed *me*. Don't let this happen to you!

MEALWORMS AND WAXWORMS

Both mealworms and waxworms can be given in supplement to green snakes but should not be offered as staple foods since neither are nutritionally complete. There aren't many reports of green snakes taking either of these items in captivity, but I suspect that's because not many keepers have offered them.

You can maintain a colony of mealworms by filling a large plastic container (such as a plastic sweaterbox) with oatmeal, then dump in about 200 adult mealworms (which can be purchased at many pet shops). Keep the container in a dark and cool place and make sure there are a few small holes in the lid for ventilation. In time, the worms will transform into black, hard-

PHOTO BY MICHAEL GILROY

The adult form of the mealworm is the Flour Beetle, *Tenebrio molitor*. Every now and then a green snake will accept these black, hard-shelled insects. However, most keepers will want to save them in order to keep their mealworm culture going.

shelled adults and will breed. The turnover rate runs in intervals of a few months, so it is advised that once you get one colony going really well, you start a few more. That way, you will assure yourself a continual mealworm flow.

Waxworms are a little more difficult to maintain and breed than mealworms, so it is suggested that you simply purchase them from a pet shop as needed.

The main problem with mealworms as herptile food is that they are not nutritionally complete—they lack calcium and other vital vitamins and minerals. Thus, they should be offered only as a supplement, not as a staple.

PHOTO BY MICHAEL GILROY

BUGS (CRAWLY THINGS)

Aside from crickets, green snakes loves many other assorted "bugs" as well. You can collect them in the wild, sometimes right from your own backyard. You have to be careful of areas that have been sprayed with pesticides, however. Searching in agricultural fields, for example, is ill-advised because much of the ground will have been chemically treated.

enclosure. Spiders and hairless caterpillars should be of particular interest since green snakes love them both.

One final note here—there are a number of reliable reports of green snakes taking earthworms with great enthusiasm. Earthworms normally aren't thought of in connection with green snakes, and yet they've been mentioned more than once. So, while you're out there with

PHOTO BY ISABELLE FRANCAIS

Mealworms can be maintained in large containers filled with grain, oats, or similar. They are best kept fairly cool (not cold, however) and in relative darkness.

In order to collect bugs, you need to run a sweep net across tall grasses and over the tops of shrubs and so forth, then transfer your catches to a jar, bring them home, and dump them into the tank. Don't capture too many critters at once or else you'll end up having to put them in their own

your sweep net unburdening the world of little creatures that most people slap or swat, lift a few wet boards or dig through piles of wet leaves for a handful of earthworms as well.

VITAMIN SUPPLEMENTS

Even the healthiest captive green snake should be given

PHOTO BY PAUL FREED

Caterpillars, particularly the hairless varieties, are much-loved by both species of green snake. They make a nutritious meal and can be collected in the field during the warmer parts of the year.

PHOTO BY MARK SMITH

PHOTO BY GUIDO DINGERKUS

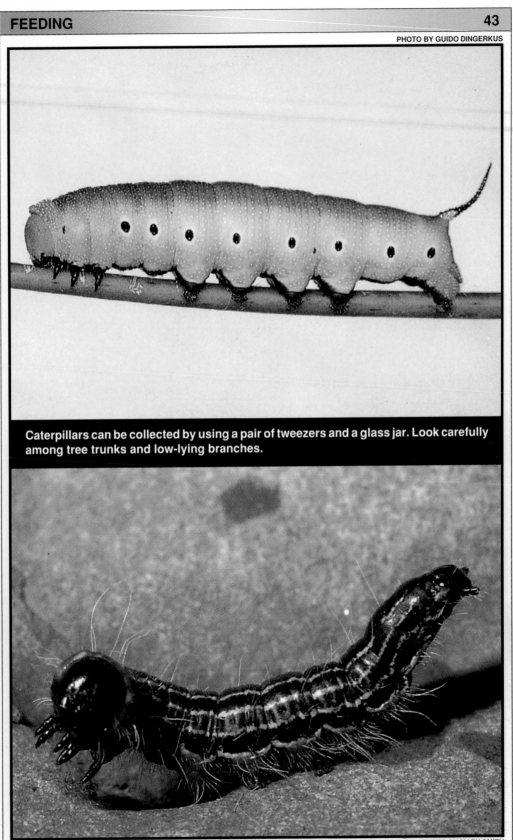

Caterpillars can be collected by using a pair of tweezers and a glass jar. Look carefully among tree trunks and low-lying branches.

PHOTO BY MARK SMITH

some sort of multivitamin supplement every now and then. These can be can be offered either in liquid or powder form. I really don't know if either form is superior. I prefer the powder only because it's easier to apply to a green snake's food items. For example, I'll place a few crickets into a plastic bag, then put in a pinch or two of powder, then shake until the crickets are completely "dusted."

Vitamin supplements need not be offered every feeding; every third or fourth is fine, and even then don't use too much. Overdoing it can have terrible consequences, sometimes leading an animal to an early death.

HOW MUCH FOOD AND HOW OFTEN?

When it comes to feeding a green snake, how much food is enough? How much is too little? Too much? Just enough?

What it comes down to is a judgment call, and it depends on a variety of subtle things. For example, some snakes seem to eat just enough food to keep them going and no more, whereas others seem like they'll keep eating until they burst. You should be careful not to indulge the latter because overfeeding is, in many ways, as dangerous as underfeeding.

Also, you must consider the size and age of the snake. Smaller snakes need to eat more frequently because they're in their tender growing years. Then again, larger snakes will take

Grasshoppers, like crickets, are a favorite food of green snakes. They rarely are domestically cultured, however, so you will have to collect them from the field. Again, avoid areas that have been treated with pesticides. Photo by Michael Gilroy.

PHOTO BY MICHAEL GILROY

Variety is the key to an effective herptile diet, so give your green snakes as many different items as they will take. Bugs like this locust may be bothersome to acquire, but in the end you will have a snake that is the very model of health.

One advantage to culturing your own mealworms is that you'll always have tiny specimens on hand to feed to your newborn green snakes, which also are very tiny. Newborn green snakes should be fed every second or third day.

PHOTO BY ISABELLE FRANCAIS

larger meals, but not as often. There really aren't any hard-and-fast rules about this, you just have to make good guesses. A newborn green snake probably should be given a handful of tiny crickets or bugs every second day (unless, of course, there still are some running around the enclosure). With adults, the same deal applies— when there aren't any prey items left, add a few more; not too many, just a few. Give them whatever you feel will satisfy them.

CAPTIVE BREEDING

Neither species of green snake has been bred in captivity with any regularity. This is not to say doing it is impossible, but green snakes don't garner enough profit to interest any of the large-scale breeders, so it simply doesn't get *tried* very often.

The propagation of *any* animal being kept in captivity is something that should at least be attempted. There is some logic to the prediction that many animals someday may exist solely in captivity, and while I don't really believe either of the *Opheodrys* species presently are threatened by this possibility, attempts to breed them still should be made. Besides, the successful breeding of any captive animal is very exciting and gives a sense of constructive purpose to our hobby.

The procedure involved in breeding green snakes is much the same as it is for most North American colubrids—a short hibernation period, ensuing copulation, gestation, the laying of eggs, and then their hatching. As you may have guessed, all the snakes discussed herein are oviparous (egglayers), so a keeper will have to deal with the many intricacies involved in successful snake-egg incubation.

CHOOSING THE BEST SPECIMENS

Healthy snakes are a vital component to a captive-breeding program. Those that are unhealthy not only won't produce viable eggs, they may not even survive the required term of hibernation.

Most of the requirements are obvious. Potential breeder snakes need to be well-fed, free of any

Green snake eggs are best incubated in a plastic shoebox containing a bedding of moistened vermiculite. If possible, separate the eggs before they have a chance to adhere to each other. That way, if one goes bad, it won't infect the rest of the clutch.

PHOTO BY W. P. MARA

obvious health problems, and fairly accustomed to captive life; stressed snakes, in spite of their steady health, probably won't breed. They also have to be sexually mature (obviously) and of compatible size.

Keep all this in mind when

hibernation process is, in a sense, a recharging period for a snake's sexual hormones. Unhibernated snakes may still breed, but the eggs, if any are laid, won't be any good.

Preparing the snakes is the first step. Hibernating snakes must be

PHOTO BY W. P. MARA

A bad snake egg as compared to a good one. Bad eggs yellow and quickly develop a light layer of fuzzy fungus. Such eggs should be disposed of at once.

shopping around for specimens. Even if you don't think you'll want to take a stab at breeding them at first, after a few months of successful keeping, your attitude probably will change.

HIBERNATION

All snakes that naturally occur in temperate zones need to go through a period of hibernation before they can breed. If they don't, they will be unable to produce fertile eggs. The

completely devoid of any waste material in their system. You should stop feeding them about two weeks before hibernation begins. During the last week, bathe the snakes daily for about an hour in warm water; this will loosen up all remaining fecal matter. This step is important because wastes allowed to remain in a system that has been slowed down by the hibernation process will ferment, infect the intestinal walls, and kill the host.

The ideal hibernating temperature for green snakes is between 52 and 55°F/11 and 13°C, and the ideal duration is about two months. Any less than seven weeks really is too risky, and any more than ten weeks probably is unnecessary. Ease the snakes into hibernation by slowly dropping their ambient temperature. Abruptly dropping them down to the recommended temperature will shock the daylights out of them; perhaps even kill them. Lower the temperature about five degrees each day.

The hibernation container can be any number of things, including the glass tank the snakes are normally kept in. I use large plastic sweaterboxes with a few holes drilled in the lid and bedded with a substrate of wood shavings or potting soil(the latter is closer to what they will encounter in nature). Other components include a hidebox and a small bowl of water, which, believe it or not, the snakes will drink from. The waterbowl should be emptied, and fresh water added, every week or so.

Other important points include the fact that the hibernaculum should be kept in a dark and quiet place. Hibernating snakes should not experience any sort of photoperiod nor should they be subjected to noise. A cellar or an attic is a good place to hibernate snakes. The only time you should disturb them is to change their water or check up on their health. Needless to say, if you notice one of the snakes losing weight at a rapid rate, remove it from hibernation, warm it back up to its normal temperature, and begin feeding it again.

After the hibernation term, increase the snakes' ambient temperature in the same gradual fashion you lowered it. Allow the snakes a day or two to reorient themselves, then try giving food.

PHOTO BY ISABELLE FRANCIS

An efficient incubator can be made by using a glass jar with a deep layer of substrate. The one shown also has a few sensors wired to it (for temperature and humidity).

MATING

It's easy getting snakes to mate as long as they've been properly conditioned—just place a male and a female together. It really is this easy. In a normal situation, the male will begin rubbing himself against the female (probably in jerky' almost spasmodic movements), then crawl along her back while twisting his tail around hers. There's always the chance that the female may not be receptive at

PHOTO BY ISABELLE FRANCAIS

Some incubators are enormous and highly complicated contraptions adorned with all sorts of bells, whistles, gauges, and wires. While such incubators could probably successfully hatch a clutch of Easter eggs, they are too expensive for most hobbyists.

bedding of moistened vermiculite, sphagnum moss, or a combination of both. All you have to do is place the box into the female's enclosure. Leave the box's lid on and make sure there's a hole drilled through it large enough for the female to squirm through. Without an egglaying box, a gravid female probably will lay her eggs in some dry corner of the enclosure, and then they'll go bad.

INCUBATION

An egglaying box can also be used as an incubator. Two important points to remember—be sure the substrate is moist (not wet, just moist), and don't turn snake eggs. By doing so you probably will kill the embryos. Also be sure some the incubation container has fresh air circulation. A few small holes in the lid will suffice (be sure you seal the mother's entrance hole because it probably will be *too* large for air circulation). Moisten the substrate (which should be checked at least every other day) by use of a spray bottle and some warm water, but

first, but after a time she should calm down, lift her own tail, and allow the male to insert of of two hemipenes. Copulation may take awhile, so be prepared. With green snakes, it normally doesn't last over an hour, but there are exceptions.

I've been asked whether or not a pair of mating snakes are distracted by human observers. Well, I've witnessed many matings and never once have the snakes been bothered by it. It certainly is a fascinating sight, and one you won't see often in your life, but overall I'd say just play it safe and don't hang around the enclosure while copulation is taking place. At the very least, observe from afar.

PREPARATIONS FOR EGGLAYING

When a gravid female becomes swollen during the last few weeks of gestation (during which time she may refuse food, which is normal), you need to provide something called a egglaying box. This can be a plastic shoe or sweaterbox with a

Small clutches of eggs that you want to incubate individually can be placed in a deli cup bedded with the appropriate substrate.

BOTH PHOTOS BY ISABELLE FRANCAIS

Large-scale snake breeding is a fun hobby that easily can turn into a part-time business. Green snakes, while not the most commercially viable animals, are good snakes to "practice" with. They also are ideal for young herpers who are trying snake-breeding for the first time.

BOTH PHOTOS BY ISABELLE FRANCAIS

The three most important climatic considerations when incubating snake eggs are temperature, humidity, and moistness of the bedding. These should be checked every day (every other day at the least) and adjusted as necessary. The substrate can be moistened through the use of a spray bottle. Use lukewarm water, and make sure you don't spray the eggs directly.

remember not to mist the eggs themselves. Getting them wet may cause them to spoil.

75°F/24°C is an ideal temperature for incubating green snake eggs. As I mentioned in the reproduction section of the natural history chapter, duration of incubation varies between the species. For the Rough Green, *aestivus*, it usually lasts between five and 12 weeks, whereas with the Smooth Green, *vernalis*, it can last only four days, with the normal being somewhere around 21 days.

At hatching time, you should see little snouts sticking up through the shell slits. You also might see the newborns crawling around with their umbilical cords still attached. Some keepers seem to have a powerful desire to "help" the snakes by snipping this. Don't, because you very well might kill them. Just be patient. The cord will detach on its own. Remember, these creatures have been culturing themselves a lot longer than you have.

NEONATAL CARE

Newborn green snakes can be housed together with no problems, (unlike the young of some species that often eat each other). Your primary concern should be getting the neonates (newborns) eating. Most will take tiny crickets (pinhead size) without fuss, but some may only take little bugs collected from the wild. it should be noted that the prey-capture techniques of the young are somewhat inefficient, so you may have to break off the large hind legs of any crickets in order to immobilize them. They'll still be able to move around (thus inspiring the required feeding response in the little snakes), but they won't be able to hop. Whether or not newborn green snakes accept freshly killed crickets is unknown to me for I have never tried it, but it's worth attempting.

PHOTO BY JIM MERLI

Some keepers like to drape some moistened sphagnum moss around a clutch of snake eggs as an additive to the vermiculite. Records suggest that doing this does in fact help maintain the moisture level.

Chances are you're going to have to wait until each snake has undergone its first shed before it will accept any food, but this should happen within ten days. Once the snakes are comfortable in their surroundings and eating regularly, you only need to sit back and watch them grow. They should reach sexual maturity in under two years (with proper and efficient care, of course), and then you'll be able to breed them just as you did their parents!

PHOTO BY JIM MERLI

Snake eggs must be handled very carefully, and most importantly, they *should not be turned from the position in which they were laid*. Doing so will kill the embryos. Once you've put the eggs in place, don't move them unless absolutely necessary.

MISCELLANEOUS TOPICS

The problem with writing a book like this is that there are lots of little things you want to say that really don't fit into the standard "feeding/breeding/housing/natural history" chapter setup yet still are important enough to warrant coverage. Acquisition, for example. Where would that fit in? The housing section? No. Breeding? No. How about handling? Or record keeping? This is why a "junk-drawer" chapter is needed.

ACQUISITION OF SPECIMENS

As I said in a different section, neither of the two *Opheodrys* species are bred in captivity with any regularity, so it's pointless to search for a breeder when seeking out specimens. Maybe more people will attempt to propagate them in the future, but for now, efforts to find such people probably will be fruitless.

This is a shame, really, because captive-bred specimens of *any* herptile are infinitely better than those captured in the wild. Wild

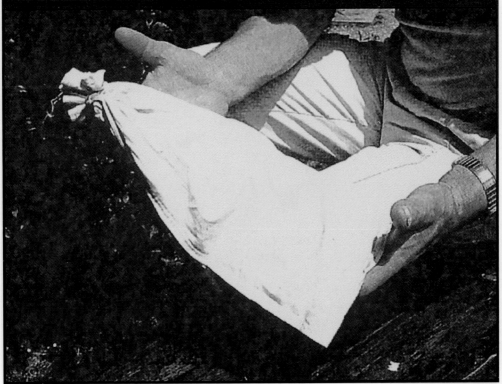

A cloth sack is perfect for transporting green snakes. Remember, however, to make sure the top is tied tight—green snakes are skilled escape artists. Also, *never* leave a sacked snake in a car where it's in the path of direct sunlight. If you do, the snake will die in a matter of *minutes*.

PHOTO BY SUSAN C. MILLER

PHOTO BY W. P. MARA

A plastic jar, like a cloth sack, is ideal for holding green snakes. Be careful when putting the lid on, however, because green snakes have a habit of abruptly lunging out of holding containers. You wouldn't want to catch one between the rim and the lid!

specimens 1) have a greater chance of carrying parasites (both internal and external, but particularly internal, which is why all new speciemns should be checked out by a vet), 2) often cannot adjust to the confines of captive life, and 3) worst of all, sometimes harbor illnesses that easily can spread to the rest of your collection.

Nevertheless, since green snakes are virtually never cultured, other routes must be taken. Your local pet shop should carry one of the two species or, at the very least, be able to order them. It is a general rule of authors not to discuss monetary values since prices of things tend to fluctuate so much.

(I'll write that green snakes cost no more than ten bucks, then next week they'll jump to fifty or sixty and everyone'll be on my back.) Let's just say green snakes have remained remarkably affordable for many, many years; around the same price as the average garter, ribbon, or water snake. The point is, if you really want to get into the keeping of green snakes, expect to spend very little money on the livestock. This is yet *another* benefit of keeping these wonderful creatures.

Finally, carefully inspect all specimens before actually making a purchase. Look for any obvious signs of illness—a runny nose, watery eyes, skin blisters, bumps under the skin, missing scales, skinniness, lethargy (listlessness), etc. Ask the dealer if you can watch the snake eat and, out of courtesy, offer to pay for the food item if the snake takes it. Use your common sense plus the knowledge you've garnered from this and other books to decide whether or not the snake you want is in good shape.

HANDLING

One of the most satisfying characteristics of the green snakes is their unbelievable benevolence. Even the squirmiest specimens seem to have no interest in striking. Wouldn't it be nice if all snakes were this way?

Of course, there always are exceptions, and even if the specimens you own are nothing more than a little wiry, you still should make some effort to accustom them to your touch.

This can be accomplished quite easily simply by handling them on a regular basis. Lift them gently out of their enclosures, making sure you give them as much

Surprise! This is *not* one of the *Opheodrys* green snakes, although it certainly does look like one. In fact, it is the Southeastern Green Snake, *Philothamnus hoplogaster*, from Africa.

PHOTO BY R. D. BARTLETT

bodily support as possible, and carry them around for a while. About a half an hour every other day should do the trick. If one does try to bite, wear a pair of rubber kitchen gloves (the taste of which seems to repulse most snakes). In time, even the most vicious specimen should become totally docile.

BEWARE OF THE MILDLY VENOMOUS GREEN SNAKES!

Can you actually believe there are venomous green snakes? I'm not talking about either of the species discussed in this book; let me assure you that both *aestivus* and *vernalis* are utterly harmless to humans. However, certain Asian "green snakes" are potentially harmful and are easily confused with the North American greens.

Why am I even mentioning this? Because, believe it or not, specimens of the aforementioned Asian green snakes sometimes end up in the same pet stores as our beloved *Opheodrys* under the *same common names*. Don't blame the retailers, they can't tell the difference. Superficially, the Asian ones really do look like those from North America. But you really should know how to tell one from the other.

The easiest ways to do this is to 1) ask for locality data (specimens collected from the United States are safe, those from Asia merely *might* be), 2) know how to

This is another *Opheodrys* twin. It is the Brazilian Green Racer, *Philodryas aestivus*, a rear-fanged colubrid from South America. Every now and then it turns up in pet shops with other green snakes, so know what you're buying before you inadvertently end up with something dangerous!

PHOTO BY W. WUSTER

positively identify *Opheodrys*, and 3) watch them eat—none of the potentially harmful "green snakes" should be willing to eat crickets. Also, most of the Asian greens grow to a larger size than those in the genus *Opheodrys*.

THE ART OF RECORD KEEPING

I did a short article in the first issue of TFH's *Reptile Hobbyist* magazine called "Hey, Write That Down!" (with the subtitle "The Art of Record Keeping") in which I rambled on for a few paragraphs about how important it is to keep careful records of all your animals' doings. This really is something I feel very strongly about, mainly because I diligently keep records myself and now, after building up a good two decades' worth of information, I'm glad I went to the trouble. It's fascinating to read over these notes and spot the patterns that have taken shape—when your snakes went through a prolific eating cycle or when they laid eggs and when those eggs hatched, etc. You end up learning a lot about the animals you keep, which is good. A keeper should become as familiar with his or her stock as possible.

Write down anything you feel is important—feedings, breedings, sheddings, defecations, egglaying, hatchings, health problems, fastings, hibernations, tank cleanings, etc. Use a notebook or a journal, a microcassette recorder or a computer. Whatever it takes to do it, do it. I like to use the huge desk calendars that have a separate square for each day.

I've developed a shorthand system that allows me to record everything quickly and easily. At the end of the month I tear off the sheet, fold it up, and file it away. If you ever have to bring your snakes to a vet, your captive-history catalogue will be of great value.

COMMON HEALTH PROBLEMS

Even snakes that enjoy the best of care can get sick. While there is a side of me that says, 'When this happens, take the animal to a vet rather than pretend to be one yourself,' another side cannot help but acknowledge the fact that certain minor crises can be dealt with in the home.

A small mite or tick infestation, for example, can be tackled by an intelligent and thoughtful hobbyist. With ticks, all you really need to do is remove the offending parasite and diligently medicate the remaining wound until it heals. Of course, you may have to deal with more than one tick at a time (although they rarely occur in groups of more than four or five). Also, remember that a tick must be removed *entirely*. It is quite easy to yank on one with tweezers or your thumb and forefinger and end up snapping the body from the head, leaving the latter behind. Make sure your grip is as close to the tick's head as possible. If after a "test tug" you feel the tick has too firm of a hold to be safely plucked off, dab it with a little rubbing alcohol first. That should cause it to relax its grip.

Although the idea that there are green snakes from foreign lands that look just like North American greens may seem novel and amusing, there is a very dark side to it too—a few of these "others" are venomous, and some are even *deadly*. Shown is Lichtenstein's Green Racer, *Philodryas olfersi*, which is known to have caused human fatalities. Photo by W. Wuster.

Mites are a little more difficult to deal with. Once an infestation is spotted, you should immediately remove the enclosure, occupants and all, to a separate area (so the infestation doesn't get the chance to spread to other enclosures). Then remove the waterbowl from the infested enclosure and put in a plastic container containing a small piece of pest strip. The container should have a few small holes drilled through it so the strip can take effect, but the holes shouldn't be so large that the snakes can have contact with the strip. The reason for the removal of the waterbowl is because pest strip will taint water, rendering it toxic.

This "pest-strip" method should take effect within a few hours. The strip should be left in the enclosure for about six hours a day for a full week. During times when the strip is not in the enclosure, the waterbowl should be put back so the snakes can drink. Once the one-week term has ended, clean the enclosure very thoroughly, wait another week, and then put the strip in again for further five days to kill off any newly hatched mites.

Minor sores, cuts, burns, and so on can be handled much in the

Don't buy any green snakes until you're absolutely sure they are of the genus *Opheodrys*, native only to the United States, southern Canada, and northern Mexico. Bringing any other slender greenish snakes, like this Miranda Green Racer, *Philodryas mattogrossensis*, into your home is a risk that isn't worth taking.

PHOTO BY PAUL FREED

same way as with humans, through the application of a little peroxide and maybe some antibiotic gel or cream. More serious is a disease common to captive snakes known as mouth rot or infectious stomatitis. The symptoms are easy to spot—the gums will be swollen, the teeth will be soft, and the snake will

off. You should be diligent about taking care of this problem because pieces left on long enough will cause skin infections and, in the case of the eye caps (also known as the "brilles"), could cause blindness.

The easy way to deal with stuck-on skin is to rub it with mineral oil, wait a few moments,

PHOTO BY W. P. MARA

Minor wounds like this one can be treated with an over-the-counter gel or creme. Larger wounds may require suturing and should be treated only by a veterinarian.

have trouble closing its mouth. One of the common causes is a severe lack of vitamin C. If you catch mouth rot in its early stages, it can be cured with a diluted (3 %) solution of hydrogen peroxide applied to the infected region with a cotton swab twice a day for about a week. The treatment then should gradually decrease as the disease tapers off. Also, the patient's vitamin C intake should be increased via a powder or liquid supplement.

Shedding problems occur quite often and almost always can be taken care of by the average hobbyist. The basic problem is pieces of old skin that, for one reason or another, refuse to come

then pinch and peel. Adherent skin also can be removed simply by bathing the snake in warm water for a few moments and then removing the skin manually (keeping the snake submerged— except for the head of course— while doing so).

Finally, let me just say that *any* health problem that has reached an advanced stage should be handled only by a professional veterinarian. I am not a vet nor do I pretend to be, and what I've written in this chapter comes strictly from firsthand experience. Don't operate out of your depth when dealing with any of the aforementioned problems or you'll end up causing your snakes more harm than good.